enough.

LIVING A LIFE BEYOND PERFORMANCE

STUDY GUIDE

Copyright © 2024 by Ben Dailey and Travis Hall

Published by Arrows & Stones

All rights reserved. No portion of this book may be reproduced, stored in a retrieval system, or transmitted in any form or by any means—electronic, mechanical, photocopy, recording, scanning, or other—except for brief quotations in critical reviews or articles, without prior written permission of the author.

Unless otherwise noted, all Scripture quotations are taken from the ESV® Bible (The Holy Bible, English Standard Version®), copyright © 2001 by Crossway, a publishing ministry of Good News Publishers. Used by permission. All rights reserved.

For foreign and subsidiary rights, contact the author.

Cover design by Kim Dailey
Ben Dailey photo by Morgan Archer
Travis Hall photo by Lyndsey Hobby

ISBN: 978-1-957369-63-1   1 2 3 4 5 6 7 8 9 10

Printed in the United States of America

enough.

LIVING A LIFE BEYOND PERFORMANCE
STUDY GUIDE

BEN DAILEY & TRAVIS HALL

ARROWS &
STONES

CONTENTS

PART 1: I'VE HAD ENOUGH!
- CHAPTER 1. This Can't Be Real!......8
- CHAPTER 2. Get on the Right Cycle!......12
- CHAPTER 3. Enough Is Enough!... Luther's Perspective......16
- CHAPTER 4. Enough Is Enough!... Paul's Take......22
- CHAPTER 5. Take Off the Mask!......28
- CHAPTER 6. No Need for a Mask!......34

PART 2: ENOUGH?
- CHAPTER 7. Am I Really Loved?......40
- CHAPTER 8. What's the Measure of Love?......46
- CHAPTER 9. Am I Really Accepted?......52
- CHAPTER 10. How Far In?......58
- CHAPTER 11. Am I Really a Son?......64
- CHAPTER 12. How Secure Am I?......70

PART 3: ENOUGH...
- CHAPTER 13. Affirmed, But......78
- CHAPTER 14. I Can Affirm Them, But......84
- CHAPTER 15. Family, But......90
- CHAPTER 16. Feeling Stuck, But......96
- CHAPTER 17. Friends, But......102
- CHAPTER 18. Not Them, But......108

PART 4: ENOUGH.
- CHAPTER 19. Exposing Wounds from the Past......116
- CHAPTER 20. Healed from Unresolved Pain......120
- CHAPTER 21. Healed from Rejection......126
- CHAPTER 22. The Pain and Power of Forgiveness......132
- CHAPTER 23. Healed from "Next."......138

PART 1:
I'VE HAD ENOUGH!

CHAPTER 1

THIS CAN'T BE REAL!

Deceiving others becomes a habit when we've deceived ourselves so much and for so long that we aren't sure what's true any longer.

READING TIME

As you read Chapter 1: "This Can't Be Real!" in *Enough.*, review, reflect on, and respond to the text by answering the following questions.

REVIEW, REFLECT, AND RESPOND:

What were Travis's initial thoughts and expectations when he attended the leadership event at Calvary? How did his assumptions shape his perception of the experience?

_____
_____
_____
_____
_____

Explore Travis's guardedness and skepticism towards Ben and the people at Calvary. Why was he initially skeptical, and how did Ben's actions challenge or confirm his suspicions?

_____
_____
_____
_____

Reflect on Travis's struggle with the performance-driven identity and the creation of a persona to meet expectations. Have you ever felt similar?

_____
_____
_____
_____
_____

Travis struggled with feeling "less than" despite his efforts. How does the performance-driven mindset affect individuals in a world of constant comparison? In what ways does this impact one's ability to accept God's grace?

_____
_____
_____
_____
_____
_____
_____
_____
_____

What are some reasons why being performance-driven instead of grace-led is so common?

_____
_____
_____
_____
_____
_____
_____
_____
_____

What are different ways trying to perform well enough to be accepted affects people? How has it affected you?

_____
_____
_____
_____
_____
_____
_____
_____
_____
_____
_____
_____
_____

What do you hope to get out of this book?

_____
_____
_____
_____
_____
_____
_____
_____
_____
_____
_____
_____
_____

CHAPTER 2

GET ON THE RIGHT CYCLE!

For believers, there are two very different ways to live: the cycle of never enough . . . and the cycle of enough.

READING TIME

As you read Chapter 2: "Get on the Right Cycle!" in *Enough.*, review, reflect on, and respond to the text by answering the following questions.

REVIEW, REFLECT, AND RESPOND:

In the text, two contrasting ways of living are presented—the cycle of never enough and the cycle of enough. How would you describe these two cycles, and how do they relate to the pursuit of significance and acceptance?

_____
_____
_____
_____
_____
_____
_____

For believers, striving isn't the problem; earning is the problem. How does this perspective challenge common notions of success and acceptance?

_____
_____
_____
_____
_____
_____
_____
_____
_____

Explore the shift in motives for living, serving, and leading that the text discusses. How does acceptance play a central role in this shift, and how does it differ from the motives driven by comparison and competition?

_____
_____
_____
_____
_____
_____

How did Ben's relational heartaches and external challenges lead him to a deeper understanding of grace? What choices did he face in dealing with his emotions and beliefs?

_____
_____
_____
_____
_____
_____

What are some of the messages of the harsh inner critic? What impact do they have?

_____
_____
_____
_____
_____

_____

_____

_____

If change comes only when we give up on unworkable strategies such as trying so hard to measure up, how close are you to that point? Explain your answer.

_____

_____

_____

_____

_____

_____

_____

On a scale of 0 (not at all) to 10 (to the max), how real has your experience of God's grace been in the past month or so?

1   2   3   4   5   6   7   8   9   10

_____

_____

_____

_____

_____

_____

_____

CHAPTER 3

ENOUGH IS ENOUGH! . . . LUTHER'S PERSPECTIVE

Those of us who haven't been captured by grace are chronically and radically insecure.

READING TIME

As you read Chapter 3: "Enough Is Enough! . . . Luther's Perspective" in Enough., review, reflect on, and respond to the text by answering the following questions.

REVIEW, REFLECT, AND RESPOND:

How does the story told at the beginning of this chapter resonate with common misconceptions about the gospel?

_____
_____
_____
_____
_____
_____
_____
_____

This chapter mentions three streams that lead to performance-based living: legalism, moralism, and human nature. How are these streams described, and how do they contribute to the struggle with self-righteousness and self-condemnation?

_____
_____
_____
_____
_____
_____
_____
_____
_____

> And when Jesus was baptized, immediately he went up from the water, and behold, the heavens were opened to him, and he saw the Spirit of God descending like a dove and coming to rest on him; and behold, a voice from heaven said, "This is my beloved son, with whom I am well pleased."
>
> —Matthew 3:16-17

Consider the scripture above and answer the following questions:

What stands out to you from this verse?

___

How does this verse reinforce the idea that acceptance precedes performance?

___

What are the manifestations of the insecurities of those who haven't fully embraced grace in terms of behavior, relationships, and self-perception? Have these manifestations ever been present in your life?

_____
_____
_____
_____
_____
_____
_____
_____
_____
_____
_____

How do the temptations Jesus experienced reflect the lies about identity, performance, and possessions?

_____
_____
_____
_____
_____
_____
_____
_____
_____
_____
_____

This chapter introduces the idea that the gospel of grace is both forensic and relational. What does this mean, and how does it impact the way believers view their relationship with God?

_____
_____
_____
_____
_____
_____
_____
_____
_____
_____

The text lists several effects of being driven by performance. Do you struggle with any of these? Which do you need to work on most?

_____
_____
_____
_____
_____
_____
_____
_____
_____
_____
_____

In our culture, how are temptations communicated to perform to meet our own needs, prove ourselves to others, and create an identity based on our wealth, intelligence, and strength? (Think of ads, commercials, songs, and other messages we hear.)

_____
_____
_____
_____
_____
_____
_____
_____
_____
_____

Look at the list of the effects of trying to get security and significance from performance. Which of these is like looking in the mirror? Are there others not listed that affect you?

_____
_____
_____
_____
_____
_____
_____
_____
_____
_____

CHAPTER 4

ENOUGH IS ENOUGH! . . . PAUL'S TAKE

Trying to earn our security and significance through our performance isn't "half a bubble" off from grace—it's the opposite of grace!

READING TIME

As you read Chapter 4: "Enough Is Enough! . . . Paul's Take" in *Enough.*, review, reflect on, and respond to the text by answering the following questions.

REVIEW, REFLECT, AND RESPOND:

How does Paul express his astonishment at the distorted gospel in Galatia, and why does he consider the alternative gospel to be contrary to the one received?

_____
_____
_____
_____
_____

Does it encourage you or discourage you that even Peter and Barnabas slid away from the truth of the gospel and tried to live by rules again? Explain your answer.

_____
_____
_____
_____
_____

Paul emphasizes the concept of justification by faith in contrast to works of the law. What does he mean by being justified by faith in Jesus Christ, and how does this relate to the performance-based identity?

_____
_____
_____
_____
_____

Paul makes a profound statement about being crucified with Christ. What does Paul mean when he makes the statement about being crucified with Christ? How does it reshape the understanding of identity and life "in Christ"?

_____
_____
_____
_____
_____
_____
_____
_____
_____
_____

Of the devastating effects of trusting in performance for security and significance discussed in this chapter, are any present in your life? Can you detect any in the lives of those close to you?

_____
_____
_____
_____
_____
_____
_____
_____
_____
_____
_____

What are some of the emotional, relational, and spiritual effects of legalism, moralism, and the bent of human nature to prove ourselves?

_____
_____
_____
_____
_____
_____
_____
_____
_____

> *Bring quickly the best robe, and put it on him, and put a ring on his hand, and shoes on his feet. And bring the fattened calf and kill it, and let us eat and celebrate. For this my son was dead, and is alive again; he was lost, and is found. And they began to celebrate.*
>
> —Luke 15:22-24

Consider the scripture above and answer the following questions:

What is the meaning of these verses?

_____
_____
_____
_____
_____
_____

What does this passage reveal about grace?

Who are you in the story of the two sons? Have you ever been the younger brother? The older brother?

What does it look like to come to the end of your efforts to prove yourself? Have you been there? Are you there now? Why or why not?

enough.

CHAPTER 5

TAKE OFF THE MASK!

When we live on stage, we naturally compare ourselves to other actors.

READING TIME

As you read Chapter 5: "Take Off the Mask!" in *Enough.*, review, reflect on, and respond to the text by answering the following questions.

REVIEW, REFLECT, AND RESPOND:

How is the *Masked Singer* show used in this chapter as an analogy for the masks people wear in their daily lives, and why is being fully known a challenge?

_____
_____
_____
_____
_____

Explain the difference between transparency and vulnerability. Why are both essential in building authentic relationships?

_____
_____
_____
_____
_____

How does the fear of rejection impact relationships, and how can finding trustworthy individuals help overcome this fear? Have you ever struggled with the fear of rejection?

_____
_____
_____
_____
_____
_____
_____

How does comparison affect our identity and relationships? How can you stop yourself from com-parison?

What are the two purposes of masks provided in this chapter?

This chapter highlights God's intimate knowledge of individuals and relates it to His love. Discuss the implications of being fully known by God and still fully loved (drawing from Psalm 139 and 1 John 3).

> *When I was a child, I spoke like a child, I thought like a child, I reasoned like a child. When I became a man, I gave up childish ways. For now we see in a mirror dimly, but then face to face. Now I know in part; then I shall know fully, even as I have been fully known.*
>
> —1 Corinthians 13:11-12

Consider the scripture above and answer the following questions:

What stands out to you from this passage?

_____
_____
_____
_____
_____
_____
_____
_____
_____

What do these verses reveal about your identity?

_____
_____
_____
_____
_____
_____
_____
_____

What are some reasons people feel compelled to wear masks? What are the risks and rewards?

___

What are some of the masks they (and we) wear? What are they trying to hide, and what are they trying to project?

___

Complete this sentence: If people really knew me, they'd. . . .

___

How does it make you feel that God knows absolutely everything about you?

___

CHAPTER 6

NO NEED FOR A MASK!

Victory isn't our ability to give God a perfect life; it's receiving His perfect love!

READING TIME

As you read Chapter 6: "No Need for a Mask!" in *Enough.*, review, reflect on, and respond to the text by answering the following questions.

REVIEW, REFLECT, AND RESPOND:

Based on Ben's story at the beginning of this chapter, how has his perspective on wearing masks changed, and what role has the gospel of grace played in this transformation?

_____
_____
_____
_____
_____
_____
_____
_____
_____

Discuss how Romans 8:31-39 reinforces the idea that God's love is unwavering and unconditional.

_____
_____
_____
_____
_____
_____
_____
_____
_____
_____

Explain how the Samaritan woman's encounter with Jesus at the well relates to the theme of being fully known and loved. How it can serve as an example for us?

_____
_____
_____
_____
_____

Affirmation based on performance can be addictive. Discuss the dangers of seeking validation through success and how this addiction can impact one's identity. Have you ever pursued this kind of validation?

_____
_____
_____
_____
_____

Explore the idea that setbacks and delays might be God's way of shaping your heart and identity. What setbacks or delays do you feel God may have employed in your life to shape your identity?

_____
_____
_____
_____
_____

Which of the passages in this chapter about God's love mean the most to you? Explain your answer.

Who is one person you can trust enough to at least be transparent about one fact you haven't wanted people to know? Is there anyone with whom you can be genuinely vulnerable?

How would your life be different if you were so secure in God's love that you didn't need to wear a mask any longer?

PART 2: ENOUGH?

CHAPTER 7

AM I REALLY LOVED?

The grace of God sets you free to become the version of you that Jesus created you to be!

READING TIME

As you read Chapter 7: "Am I Really Loved?" in *Enough.*, review, reflect on, and respond to the text by answering the following questions.

REVIEW, REFLECT, AND RESPOND:

Why do you think grace can be a misunderstood or controversial concept, and how does this chapter address these concerns?

_____
_____
_____
_____
_____
_____
_____
_____
_____
_____

How are grace and holiness intertwined?

_____
_____
_____
_____
_____
_____
_____
_____
_____
_____

What is "cheap grace"? How does it differ from the biblical understanding of grace?

___

What is the difference between religion and love? Discuss their distinctions and how they reflect the difference between a legalistic approach and the true nature of God's love.

___

The Parable of the Good Samaritan is discussed as an illustration of fully knowing and fully loving someone. How does this parable challenge traditional views and expectations, and what does it reveal about God's love?

___

How would you describe the impact of a stable, loving family with "good enough" parents on a person's self-concept, motivations, and image of God?

How would you describe the impact a chaotic home has on a child? What about a home where at least one parent was emotionally or physically distant?

> *O righteous Father, even though the world does not know you, I know you, and these know that you have sent me. I made known to them your name, and I will continue to make it known, that the love with which you have loved me may be in them, and I in them.*
>
> —John 17:25-26

Consider the scripture above and answer the following questions:

What do these verses reveal about God the Father?

_____
_____
_____
_____
_____
_____
_____
_____

Think through the Gospels. What are some ways Jesus accurately depicted the Father's character?

_____
_____
_____
_____
_____
_____
_____
_____

enough.

CHAPTER 8

WHAT'S THE MEASURE OF LOVE?

Who we are is determined by our view of God, and our view of God is shaped by our earliest and most important relationships.

READING TIME

As you read Chapter 8: "What's the Measure of Love?" in Enough., review, reflect on, and respond to the text by answering the following questions.

REVIEW, REFLECT, AND RESPOND:

Why has grace become controversial in some Christian circles, especially in holiness traditions?

_____
_____
_____
_____
_____
_____

How does this chapter challenge the common perception of grace as a temporary, optional movement?

_____
_____
_____
_____
_____
_____

What are the three warnings mentioned in the holiness tradition?

_____
_____
_____
_____
_____
_____

Why is the notion that grace promotes sin a misconception?

_____

_____

_____

_____

_____

_____

_____

_____

_____

_____

_____

_____

What is "New Covenant grace"?

_____

_____

_____

_____

_____

_____

_____

_____

_____

_____

_____

_____

Which of the false images of God do you see in some family and friends? Where do you think they got these concepts?

Look again at the story from *A Tale of Two Cities*. How does it affect you to see yourself as Darnay? As the woman in the cart with Carton?

> *. . . so that Christ may dwell in your hearts through faith—that you, being rooted and grounded in love, may have strength to comprehend with all the saints what is the breadth and length and height and depth, and to know the love of Christ that surpasses knowledge, that you may be filled with the fullness of God.*
>
> —Ephesians 3:17-19

Consider the scripture above and answer the following questions:

What is the meaning of this passage?

_____
_____
_____
_____
_____
_____
_____

What do these verses reveal about the love of Christ?

_____
_____
_____
_____
_____
_____
_____

What are some differences between intellectually knowing God loves you and experiencing His love?

Do you have some fears, doubts, and pride in performance that are hindering your experience of God's great love for you? (We all do.) What are they? How does God's love overcome your resistance?

CHAPTER 9

AM I REALLY ACCEPTED?

We didn't earn our acceptance and sons and daughters. . . . It's a free gift.

READING TIME

As you read Chapter 9: "Am I Really Accepted?" in *Enough.*, review, reflect on, and respond to the text by answering the following questions.

REVIEW, REFLECT, AND RESPOND:

How did Ben's and Travis's understanding of grace evolve over the years, and how did it impact their preaching and interactions with people? How has your understanding of grace evolved?

_____
_____
_____
_____
_____
_____
_____

What is the significance of the desire for acceptance in the human experience, and how does the text argue that this need is not a flaw but rather a part of how God created us?

_____
_____
_____
_____
_____
_____
_____
_____
_____

How does the pressure for acceptance in the world impact individuals and their choices? Provide examples from the text that illustrate the consequences of living under this pressure.

_____
_____
_____
_____
_____
_____
_____
_____
_____
_____

How does Ben share his personal struggle with the conflicting messages about God's love during his time in Bible college? What impact did these conflicting messages have on his identity and understanding of grace?

_____
_____
_____
_____
_____
_____
_____
_____
_____
_____

In what ways does the text explain the psychological impact of rejection, comparing it to physical pain? How does unhealed rejection manifest in individuals, and why is it likened to living with a broken bone?

_____
_____
_____
_____
_____
_____
_____
_____
_____
_____

What are some symptoms of insecurity, and how do they affect individuals in their relationships and daily lives?

_____
_____
_____
_____
_____
_____
_____
_____
_____
_____

What is the solution to the performance- and fear-based acceptance mentioned in the text?

_____
_____
_____
_____
_____
_____
_____

How does the concept of being "accepted in the Beloved" emphasize the free gift of acceptance rather than something earned through performance?

_____
_____
_____
_____
_____
_____
_____

How would you describe the price people pay to be accepted by others?

_____
_____
_____

Which of the symptoms of insecurity are issues for you?

What are some reasons it's so easy to accept God's grace for our salvation but drift back into believing performance earns approval?

CHAPTER 10

HOW FAR IN?

We let people in only as far as we perceive we can trust them, and our trust is (or should be) based on their proven trustworthiness.

READING TIME

As you read Chapter 10: "How Far In?" in *Enough.*, review, reflect on, and respond to the text by answering the following questions.

REVIEW, REFLECT, AND RESPOND:

How does the concept of trust, represented as keys to doors in our lives, play a crucial role in determining how far we let people into our lives, including God?

_____
_____
_____
_____
_____
_____
_____
_____

What message does Jesus convey through His actions, especially in contrast to the Pharisees, regarding acceptance and inclusion? How does this reflect the principles of grace as outlined in the text?

_____
_____
_____
_____
_____
_____
_____
_____
_____
_____

How does the grace of God redefine an individual's status and acceptance? In what ways does grace differ from conditional acceptance, and how does it go beyond just being a ticket through the door?

_____
_____
_____
_____
_____
_____
_____
_____
_____
_____

Why does the text emphasize that acceptance by God isn't based on what individuals do but on what Jesus has already done? How might misunderstanding this concept lead to spiritual and emotional dysfunction?

_____
_____
_____
_____
_____
_____
_____
_____
_____
_____

Explain the analogy of treating God like an employer versus a father.

Explore the four gospel truths presented in this chapter for healing from past rejection and the fear of being rejected. How does each truth contribute to a more profound understanding of acceptance, forgiveness, and self-acceptance?

Why is it significant that Jesus moved toward outcasts?

_____
_____
_____
_____
_____
_____
_____
_____
_____
_____

How do past wounds shape our willingness to receive God's love and acceptance?

_____
_____
_____
_____
_____
_____
_____
_____
_____
_____

How would you summarize each of the four gospel truths at the end of the chapter?

How would the overflow of God's unconditional acceptance affect your relationships?

CHAPTER 11

AM I REALLY A SON?

The truths of God's love, His acceptance, and our status as sons and heirs aren't three distinct concepts. . . . They interlock and overlap.

READING TIME

As you read Chapter 11: "Am I Really a Son?" in *Enough*, review, reflect on, and respond to the text by answering the following questions.

REVIEW, REFLECT, AND RESPOND:

Explain the significance of the term "Gotcha Day" and how it parallels the concept of adoption in the Scriptures, emphasizing the unbreakable bond between God and believers as His adopted children.

_____
_____
_____
_____
_____
_____
_____
_____

Identify and discuss the signs of chronic inferiority as outlined in the text, such as rampant comparison, hypersensitivity to criticism, catastrophizing, black-and-white thinking, and perfectionism. How do these signs manifest in the lives of individuals struggling with chronic inferiority?

_____
_____
_____
_____
_____
_____
_____
_____

Share the personal experiences of Travis and Ben in dealing with feelings of inferiority, comparison, and competition. How did the revelation of God's grace transform their perspectives, relationships, and self-perception?

_____
_____
_____
_____
_____

Explore the role of grace in healing chronic inferiority and the pursuit of self-worth through performance. How do the New Covenant and God's unmerited grace serve as powerful tools for overcoming deep-seated insecurities?

_____
_____
_____
_____
_____

Reflect on the impact of comparison and competition on relationships, as described in the personal experiences of the authors. How did the revelation of being beloved sons in Christ change their interactions and perspectives on relationships?

_____
_____
_____
_____
_____

> *For in Christ Jesus you are all sons of God, through faith. For as many of you as were baptized into Christ have put on Christ. There is neither Jew nor Greek, there is neither slave nor free, there is no male and female, for you are all one in Christ Jesus. And if you are Christ's, then you are Abraham's offspring, heirs according to promise.*
>
> —Galatians 3:26-29

Consider the passage above and answer the following questions:

What do these verses reveal about our equality?

_____
_____
_____
_____
_____
_____

Explore the idea that the challenge to grasp the concept of sonship isn't exclusive to women but also extends to men, primarily due to issues of inferiority. How do the truths of God's love, acceptance, and our status as sons and heirs intertwine?

_____
_____
_____
_____
_____
_____

How do you think the people in the churches of Galatia responded when they read Paul's statement: "There is neither Jew nor Greek, there is neither slave nor free, there is no male and female, for you are all one in Christ Jesus"?

_____
_____
_____
_____
_____
_____

How would you define inferiority? What forms does it take in people's lives?

_____
_____
_____
_____
_____
_____

Which of the signs of chronic inferiority can you relate to? Explain your answer.

_____
_____
_____
_____
_____
_____

enough.

CHAPTER 12

HOW SECURE AM I?

Our status as sons of the King is the antidote to the poison of inferiority.

READING TIME

As you read Chapter 12: "How Secure Am I?" in *Enough.*, review, reflect on, and respond to the text by answering the following questions.

REVIEW, REFLECT, AND RESPOND:

Explain how our status as "sons of the King" serves as an antidote to the poison of inferiority, emphasizing the transformative power of being "in Christ." How does this status change our perspective on past mistakes?

_____
_____
_____
_____
_____
_____
_____
_____

Discuss the tactics used by the enemy to keep believers from recognizing their new identity as sons. How can believers combat these accusations and stand firm in the truth of their acceptance and status in Christ?

_____
_____
_____
_____
_____
_____
_____
_____

Analyze the metaphor of siege warfare in 2 Corinthians 10:3-5, describing the battle for our minds and hearts. What weapons has God provided to believers in this spiritual battle, and how can they use truth and faith to overcome strongholds?

_____
_____
_____
_____
_____

Elaborate on the unique identity believers have in Christ, contrasting it with the world's standards. How does the Holy Spirit's seal assure believers of their unshakable relationship with the Father?

_____
_____
_____
_____
_____

Discuss the idea that as sons, believers have a role in expanding God's kingdom "on earth as it is in heaven." How does the concept of delegated authority replace feelings of inferiority with royal authority?

_____
_____
_____
_____
_____

Explore the courtroom analogy, emphasizing the role of Jesus as our defense attorney. How does the truth of being forgiven and claimed by God counteract the accusations and condemnations often faced by believers?

_____
_____
_____
_____
_____
_____

What does it mean to live like "the jury is still out, and the verdict is still in doubt"? Can you relate to that pressure and fear?

_____
_____
_____
_____
_____
_____

Compare the stories of the younger and older sons from Jesus's parable, illustrating how feelings of inferiority and superiority can impact one's understanding of sonship. How can believers avoid the pitfalls of arrogance and self-righteousness and embrace their identity as beloved sons?

_____
_____
_____
_____
_____
_____

Read Packer's quote again. What stands out to you? Ask God to make it real to your heart that you are His beloved son.

___

> *From now on, therefore, we regard to no one according to the flesh. Even though we once regarded Christ according to the flesh, we regard him thus no longer. Therefore, if anyone is in Christ, he is a new creation. The old has passed away; behold, the new has come.*
>
> —2 Corinthians 5:16-17

Consider the scripture above and answer the following questions:

What is the meaning of this passage?

___

What does Paul mean by "according to the flesh"?

What does it mean that we are "new creations"? In what way are we new?

PART 3: ENOUGH . . .

CHAPTER 13

AFFIRMED, BUT . . .

We couldn't give what we didn't possess, but now we possess the affirmation of God, and it possesses us!

READING TIME

As you read Chapter 13: "Affirmed, But . . ." in *Enough.*, review, reflect on, and respond to the text by answering the following questions.

REVIEW, REFLECT, AND RESPOND:

Why is it essential for believers to recognize and internalize God's affirmations towards them, and how does this recognition transform their relationships with others?

_____
_____
_____
_____
_____
_____
_____
_____

How do childhood experiences, particularly in the early years, shape an individual's ability to give and receive affirmation? Discuss the impact of neglect, harsh treatment, or overprotective parenting on a person's emotional well-being.

_____
_____
_____
_____
_____
_____
_____
_____

Explore the characteristics of individuals who did not experience overwhelming affirmation as children, as outlined in the chapter. How do these characteristics manifest in their emotions, relationships, and overall outlook on life?

_____
_____
_____
_____
_____
_____
_____
_____
_____

Discuss the challenges believers face when bringing their emotional baggage into their new relationship with God. How does the gospel play a role in healing deep wounds and replacing old hurts with God's kindness, compassion, and delight?

_____
_____
_____
_____
_____
_____
_____
_____
_____

Reflect on the encounter between Jesus and the leper as described in Mark 1:40-42. What does this passage reveal about Jesus's compassion, and how does it challenge conventional societal norms of that time?

_____
_____
_____
_____
_____
_____
_____
_____
_____
_____

Analyze the story of the woman who anointed Jesus's feet, contrasting the Pharisee's judgment with Jesus's affirmation. How does Jesus defend and affirm the woman, breaking societal norms and highlighting the power of forgiveness and love?

_____
_____
_____
_____
_____
_____
_____
_____
_____
_____

Imagine yourself as the leper in Mark 1 or the woman in Luke 7. What was it like for them to receive Jesus's compassion?

_____
_____
_____
_____
_____
_____
_____

Explore the three elements that Jesus consistently gave people in his interactions: attention, affirmation, and an invitation. How can believers model these elements in their relationships, and what impact can this have on the lives of those around them?

_____
_____
_____
_____
_____
_____
_____

Discuss the idea that Jesus engaged with people from all walks of life, including those who were down and out and those who were up and coming. How does this challenge common perceptions and expectations, and what does it reveal about the nature of Christ's affection and affirmation?

_____
_____

Do you agree or disagree with the description in the opening paragraphs of this chapter about the impact of parents on small children? Explain your answer.

How would you describe the impact of your home life on your self-concept, your confidence, your ability to trust wisely, and your ability to love without strings attached?

CHAPTER 14

I CAN AFFIRM THEM, BUT . . .

*Man's affirmation is supplemental;
God's is transformational*

READING TIME

As you read Chapter 14: "I Can Affirm Them, But . . ." in *Enough.*, review, reflect on, and respond to the text by answering the following questions.

REVIEW, REFLECT, AND RESPOND:

Why do some individuals find it challenging to affirm those closest to them, such as family members or close friends? Explore possible reasons mentioned in the chapter, such as insincerity, emotional withdrawal, or past disappointments.

_____
_____
_____
_____
_____
_____
_____
_____

How can insincere affirmations have a negative impact, especially in close relationships? Describe a time you've experienced this to be true.

_____
_____
_____
_____
_____
_____
_____
_____

Discuss the story told in this chapter of the woman who grew up with an insatiable craving for love due to emotional abuse. How did experiencing God's grace and participating in a small group contribute to her healing? What role did the affirmations from the women in the group play in her transformation?

_____
_____
_____
_____
_____
_____
_____
_____
_____

Explore the relational nature of human beings as highlighted in the chapter. How does the need for affirmation connect individuals on a deeper level? Provide examples, including biblical references, to support this idea.

_____
_____
_____
_____
_____
_____
_____
_____
_____
_____

Reflect on the Acts 20:36-38 passage where Paul bids farewell to the elders in Ephesus. How does this scene challenge the perception of Paul as a "go-it-alone" figure, and what does it reveal about the transformative power of affirmation in building deep connections?

_____
_____
_____
_____
_____
_____
_____
_____
_____
_____
_____

Discuss the idea that man's affirmation is supplemental, while God's affirmation is transformational. How can understanding and internalizing God's affirmation affect an individual's ability to give and receive affirmation from others?

_____
_____
_____
_____
_____
_____
_____
_____
_____
_____
_____

Pastor Frederick Buechner emphasizes the hunger to be known, understood, and loved. How does this hunger relate to the importance of affirmation, both from people and from God? In what ways can affirmation satisfy emotional hunger and contribute to healing and encouragement?

_____
_____
_____
_____
_____
_____
_____
_____
_____

Who has stepped into your life to affirm you, believe in you, and see a future for you? How was this affirmation communicated? How did you receive it?

_____
_____
_____
_____
_____
_____
_____
_____
_____

Do you agree or disagree that many of the most compassionate, insightful people were deeply wounded but experienced healing through the grace of God and the love of a few people? Explain your answer.

Who needs your words and actions of affirmation today? What difference will it make?

CHAPTER 15

FAMILY, BUT . . .

Getting hurt is inevitable, but staying hurt is optional.

READING TIME

As you read Chapter 15: "Family, But . . ." in *Enough.*, review, reflect on, and respond to the text by answering the following questions.

REVIEW, REFLECT, AND RESPOND:

How does the statement "Affirmed people affirm people, but hurt people hurt people" reflect the central theme of this chapter regarding the impact of personal wounds on our interactions with others, especially within family relationships?

_____
_____
_____
_____
_____
_____
_____

In Travis's personal story of his early marriage with Tina, what role did unhealed wounds from his past play in shaping his behavior and emotional responses within the relationship? How did these wounds contribute to a cycle of fear, insecurity, and pride?

_____
_____
_____
_____
_____
_____
_____
_____

Explore the concept that getting hurt is inevitable, but staying hurt is optional. How does the chapter suggest that unhealed wounds can perpetuate self-defeating cycles and hinder an individual's ability to give and receive love?

___

___

___

___

___

___

___

___

___

Explain the idea that "time alone doesn't heal pain—it incubates it." Provide a personal example or example from the text and discuss the consequences of allowing unresolved pain to linger over time, affecting various aspects of one's life.

___

___

___

___

___

___

___

___

___

Discuss the link between fear, insecurity, and pride and how these emotions contribute to the creation of walls around the heart. How does this self-protective mechanism impact an individual's ability to experience and express love in relationships?

_____
_____
_____
_____
_____
_____
_____
_____
_____
_____

Explore the concept of insecurity as fertile soil for a toxic form of pride. How does self-pity, in this context, become a distorted expression of pride? Discuss the difference between self-pity and a healthy acknowledgment of one's suffering.

_____
_____
_____
_____
_____
_____
_____
_____
_____
_____

Analyze the inner conflicts described in the text, such as the desire for intimacy while fearing exposure. How do these conflicts manifest in relationships, and what challenges do individuals face in breaking down the walls they've built to protect themselves?

___

What do you think it means to "lean into your pain"? Have you ever done this? If you have, what happened? If you haven't, is this a good time to start?

___

What are some of the ways our family relationships are affected by burying our wounds of the past?

Who is a safe person for you? How vulnerable are you with that person? What difference does it make?

CHAPTER 16

FEELING STUCK, BUT . . .

*Forgiving the person who hurt you begins
with a focus on God's forgiveness of you.*

READING TIME

As you read Chapter 16: "Feeling Stuck, But..." in *Enough.*, review, reflect on, and respond to the text by answering the following questions.

REVIEW, REFLECT, AND RESPOND:

How does the chapter emphasize that conflict can serve as a catalyst for healing rather than perpetuating unresolved issues? Provide examples from this chapter to illustrate this perspective.

_____
_____
_____
_____
_____
_____
_____
_____

Discuss the significance of choosing an honest moment and its role in initiating the process of healing. How does an honest moment contribute to self-reflection, especially when dealing with patterns of behavior that have persisted over the years?

_____
_____
_____
_____
_____
_____
_____
_____

Explore the steps involved in facing and grieving the source of pain. Why is it essential to confront and work through the emotional wounds rather than resorting to avoidance or temporary solutions?

_____
_____
_____
_____
_____
_____
_____
_____
_____
_____

Analyze the concept of "a geographical cure" and its limitations in addressing unresolved emotional pain. How does the chapter argue that true healing requires more than changing external circumstances?

_____
_____
_____
_____
_____
_____
_____
_____
_____
_____

Explain the role of forgiveness in the healing process. How does holding onto bitterness and resentment hinder the ability to heal, and how does forgiveness contribute to both emotional and physical well-being?

_____
_____
_____
_____
_____
_____
_____
_____
_____
_____

Discuss the importance of finding a safe person in the healing journey. How does having a trustworthy guide, such as a counselor, help individuals navigate the complexities of their emotional wounds and facilitate the process of healing?

_____
_____
_____
_____
_____
_____
_____
_____
_____
_____

Explore the idea of developing tenacious hope and its role in the healing process. How does maintaining hope contribute to perseverance and resilience during challenging times in the journey toward emotional health?

_____
_____
_____
_____
_____
_____
_____

Analyze the chapter's discussion on parenting and the impact of an individual's belief in their own "enoughness" on how they parent. How does recognizing and addressing personal insecurities positively influence the way people interact with their children?

_____
_____
_____
_____
_____
_____
_____

Review the steps outlined in this chapter. What's your next step? When and how will you take it?

_____
_____

What difference does it (or would it) make to give the messages to your children: "I love you. I'm really proud of you. And you're really good at . . ."?

Why does someone who is trying to impart grace to his or her family need tenacious hope? What stumbling blocks might be found along the way?

CHAPTER 17

FRIENDS, BUT . . .

It's only when we recognize how Christ is a friend to us, just as we are, that we're able to in turn be a good friend to others.

READING TIME

As you read Chapter 17: "Friends, But...," in *Enough.*, review, reflect on, and respond to the text by answering the following questions.

REVIEW, REFLECT, AND RESPOND:

Discuss the negative consequences of relationships based on performance and the constant need for approval. How do such dynamics lead to exhaustion, jealousy, and insecurity in friendships?

_____
_____
_____
_____
_____
_____
_____
_____
_____

Explore the concept of comparison and its impact on friendships. How does the chapter argue that the culture of comparison, especially prevalent in today's society and social media, hinders genuine connections and friendships?

_____
_____
_____
_____
_____
_____
_____
_____

Among your circle of friends, what are the points of comparison, spoken or unspoken? What impact does comparing have on these relationships?

_____
_____
_____
_____
_____
_____
_____
_____
_____
_____

Discuss the role of competition in relationships, particularly in the context of friendship. How does the scarcity mindset, driven by the belief that one's worth is never enough, contribute to competition rather than collaboration in friendships?

_____
_____
_____
_____
_____
_____
_____
_____
_____
_____

Competition is the natural result of comparison. How does competing with others affect relationships? Is competing ever good, with positive results? What's the difference between the good kind and the toxic kind?

_____
_____
_____
_____
_____
_____
_____
_____
_____

How does the experience of grace liberate individuals from the need to compare and compete? Provide insights from the text on how recognizing one's identity in Christ and understanding God's abundant love and grace transform the way people relate to others.

_____
_____
_____
_____
_____
_____
_____
_____
_____
_____

Explore the link between burnout and the relentless pursuit of comparison and competition. How does the chapter suggest that burnout is a consequence of seeking affirmation through performance and external validation?

_____
_____
_____
_____
_____
_____
_____
_____
_____
_____

How can a person tell that burnout is approaching? What are some steps to take to stop the progression?

_____
_____
_____
_____
_____
_____
_____
_____
_____
_____

Summarize the key messages that grace communicates to individuals who feel overwhelmed by the pressures of comparison, competition, and burnout. How do these messages contribute to the development of rich and meaningful friendships?

___

CHAPTER 18

NOT THEM, BUT . . .

*No buts, true friends always let you
in and never let you down.*

READING TIME

As you read Chapter 18: "Not Them, But..." in *Enough.*, review, reflect on, and respond to the text by answering the following questions.

REVIEW, REFLECT, AND RESPOND:

In what ways does the chapter emphasize the importance of finding friends who go beyond genetic connections and can be closer than family? What is the significance of the biblical quote from Proverbs 18:24 in this context?

_____
_____
_____
_____
_____
_____
_____

Explore the impact of the current cultural and political climate on friendships. How does this chapter describe the challenges posed by increased polarization and a lack of civility in society, and how can true friends navigate these differences?

_____
_____
_____
_____
_____
_____
_____
_____

Discuss the two reactions—resentment and a victim mentality—that disagreements can produce when the gospel hasn't penetrated our hearts. How does the chapter suggest that genuine friends handle disagreements, and why is active listening important in these situations?

_____
_____
_____
_____
_____
_____
_____

What practical suggestions does this chapter provide for finding and developing great friends? How can being observant, moving slowly and carefully, practicing progressive vetting, and dealing with conflicts promptly contribute to the growth of meaningful friendships?

_____
_____
_____
_____
_____
_____
_____

What are some ways to practice "progressive vetting"?

_____
_____
_____

> *A thorn was given me in the flesh, a messenger of Satan to harass me, to keep me from becoming conceited. Three times I pleaded with the Lord about this, that it should leave me. But he said to me, My grace is sufficient for you, for my power is made perfect in weakness. Therefore I will boast all the more gladly of my weaknesses, so that the power of Christ may rest upon me.*
>
> —2 Corinthians 12:7-9

Consider the scripture above and answer the following questions:

What is revealed through this passage?

Explain the connection between Paul's experience of a "thorn in the flesh" and the challenges individuals face in building and sustaining meaningful friendships.

How do you think Jesus feels about Christians today who voice as much resentment, demands, and grievance as unbelievers? When is anger justified? When is it a poor testimony?

Think of two or three memorable commercials. What were the two promises in each one: what would the product actually do, and what would it do for the user's popularity and prestige?

Which end of the spectrum (or the golden middle) do you find yourself: trusting too much too soon or unwilling to take any risk to give and receive love in a friendship? Explain your answer.

How do you see Jesus's love, acceptance, and affirmation of you impacting the way you engage with friends?

PART 4:
ENOUGH.

CHAPTER 19

EXPOSING WOUNDS FROM THE PAST.

Good deeds aren't the problem ... trusting in them to earn God's approval (and the applause of people) is a huge problem.

READING TIME

As you read Chapter 19: "Exposing Wounds from the Past." in *Enough.*, review, reflect on, and respond to the text by answering the following questions.

REVIEW, REFLECT, AND RESPOND:

What significant event in Travis's life caused him to turn away from God and engage in destructive behaviors for four years? How did this period of rebellion affect his relationship with God, and what was the turning point that led him back to faith?

_____
_____
_____
_____
_____
_____
_____

Explain how the author's encounter with legalistic beliefs about God created internal conflict and affected his spiritual journey. How did these conflicting messages contribute to his struggles with addiction, performance, and understanding God's love?

_____
_____
_____
_____
_____
_____
_____
_____

Explore Travis's realization about the addictive nature of legalistic beliefs, comparing them to the tolerance effect experienced by substance abusers. How did his performance-oriented view of God become as addictive as his previous struggles with alcohol, drugs, and sex?

_____
_____
_____
_____
_____
_____
_____

In Luke 15, what is the contrast between the two brothers' ways of salvation, and how does Travis's personal experience relate to the themes of repentance, grace, and the Father's love?

_____
_____
_____
_____
_____
_____
_____

How does the experience of God's love, forgiveness, and acceptance precede and influence a life of obedience?

_____
_____
_____

As you read this chapter, what past hurts came to mind? What have you done with those memories over the years?

Of the different sources of pain, which have you suffered?

CHAPTER 20

HEALED FROM UNRESOLVED PAIN.

You're not waiting to heal before God sees you as enough, because your wounds don't determine your worth—Jesus does.

READING TIME

As you read Chapter 20: "Healed from Unresolved Pain." in *Enough.*, review, reflect on, and respond to the text by answering the following questions.

REVIEW, REFLECT, AND RESPOND:

Explain the cycle of unresolved pain outlined in this chapter.

_____
_____
_____
_____
_____
_____
_____
_____
_____

Describe how fear, insecurity, and pride are the natural outworking of unhealed wounds. How do you see this cycle in the lives of people you know? (No names, please, and if you write, disguise the details to protect privacy.)

_____
_____
_____
_____
_____
_____
_____
_____
_____

Discuss the sources of unresolved pain, including trauma, rejection, and abuse. How does living in a fallen world contribute to the brokenness experienced by individuals? Reflect on the significance of addressing childhood hurts and the impact of catastrophic events on a person's well-being.

_____
_____
_____
_____
_____
_____
_____
_____
_____

Analyze the concept of fear as an operating system when hurt becomes the core of one's identity. What are the various fears mentioned, such as the fear of failure, rejection, losing control, not being enough, and conflict? How do these fears affect a person's freedom and ability to move forward?

_____
_____
_____
_____
_____
_____
_____
_____
_____

Explore the role of insecurity in the cycle of unresolved pain. How does self-doubt hinder individuals from reaching their sense of purpose and destiny? Discuss the manifestations of insecurity, such as comparison, competition, and masking weaknesses in relationships.

_____
_____
_____
_____
_____
_____
_____
_____
_____
_____

Examine the essence of pride in attempting to make sense of pain, fear, and insecurity. How does trusting in one's abilities contribute to the cycle of unresolved pain? Discuss the observable behaviors associated with pride, including blaming others, reacting to perceived injustices, and a lack of trust in authority.

_____
_____
_____
_____
_____
_____
_____
_____
_____
_____

Summarize the principles, practices, and processes outlined in this chapter regarding healing from unresolved pain. Why is it essential to have both insights and courage in the healing process? Discuss the common coping strategies of minimizing, excusing, and denying pain and how courageous individuals overcome deep emotional wounds.

_____
_____
_____
_____
_____

Emphasize the importance of seeking relationships in the healing journey. Why do people need the support of wise, patient, and loving individuals to navigate through the layers of pain? Discuss the role of counselors, sponsors, or friends who have experience in the healing process.

_____
_____
_____
_____
_____

Reflect on the recommendation to trust the Holy Spirit in bringing to mind the events and people that have caused pain. How can individuals overcome the repression of memories and engage in the process of remembering and documenting past hurts? Discuss the significance of patience and persistence in emotional, spiritual, and relational healing.

_____
_____

Take a few minutes now to ask the Holy Spirit to bring painful events and the people who caused them to mind. Don't excuse the people, don't minimize the impact of the events, and don't deny that it affected you. Write it down.

Think of someone you know (maybe yourself) who has suffered significant emotional wounds. What do you think the process of healing looks like? How is it like peeling an onion? Is it worth the effort? Why or why not?

CHAPTER 21

HEALED FROM REJECTION.

Rejection runs the gamut from momentary hurt feelings to devastating betrayal and catastrophic loss.

READING TIME

As you read Chapter 21: "Healed from Rejection." in *Enough.*, review, reflect on, and respond to the text by answering the following questions.

REVIEW, REFLECT, AND RESPOND:

Explore the impact of rejection on individuals, considering both momentary hurt feelings and more profound experiences like betrayal and catastrophic loss. How do the stories of Carol, Carl, and Sarah illustrate the different forms and consequences of rejection in their lives?

_____
_____
_____
_____
_____
_____
_____

Discuss the role of comparison and criticism in Carol's life and how it contributed to her development of perfectionism and obsessive-compulsive disorder. In what ways did her mother's actions shape Carol's self-perception and affect her relationships, including her marriage and parenting?

_____
_____
_____
_____
_____
_____
_____

Analyze Carl's experience of rejection due to his health condition and the subsequent impact on his choices, including seeking acceptance from the druggies. How did rejection lead him down a path of addiction, and what were the relational consequences he faced later in life?

_____
_____
_____
_____
_____
_____
_____
_____

Examine the emotional absence of Sarah's father and the perfectionism of her mother, highlighting the impact on Sarah's insecurity and her struggle to express painful emotions. How did these factors contribute to Sarah's use of food as a coping mechanism and the development of an eating disorder?

_____
_____
_____
_____
_____
_____
_____
_____

Explore the transformative power of the gospel of grace in dealing with rejection. How does the gospel provide a foundation, capability, and courage to forgive those who have hurt us and find acceptance in Christ? Share examples from the text or personal experiences that demonstrate this transformation.

_____
_____
_____
_____
_____
_____
_____
_____
_____

Discuss the challenges of offering comfort to someone experiencing rejection. Why is "reactive comforting" problematic, and how does it fail to address the complexity of life's difficult questions? Explore the importance of allowing space for grieving and processing loss before encouraging individuals to move on.

_____
_____
_____
_____
_____
_____
_____
_____
_____

Consider the analogy of a commercial passenger plane to understand the need for acknowledging and dealing with pain. How does the reluctance to face and process pain mirror society's tendency to avoid dealing with it? Discuss alternative approaches, such as distractions and avoidance, and their potential consequences.

_____
_____
_____
_____
_____
_____
_____
_____
_____
_____

Who came to mind as you read this chapter?

_____
_____
_____
_____
_____
_____
_____
_____
_____
_____
_____

enough.

CHAPTER 22

THE PAIN AND POWER OF FORGIVENESS.

Forgiveness is an integral part of our new nature because it's God's nature.

READING TIME

As you read Chapter 22: "The Pain and Power of Forgiveness." in *Enough.*, review, reflect on, and respond to the text by answering the following questions.

REVIEW, REFLECT, AND RESPOND:

Give your definition of forgiveness. What are some ways forgiveness has been misunderstood or misrepresented?

_____
_____
_____
_____
_____
_____
_____
_____
_____
_____
_____

How would you explain that forgiveness is both a choice and a process?

_____
_____
_____
_____
_____
_____
_____
_____
_____
_____
_____

What are some differences in resources and motives to forgive between the Old Covenant and the New Covenant?

_____
_____
_____
_____
_____
_____
_____

What's necessary for reconciliation to happen?

_____
_____
_____
_____
_____
_____
_____

As you read this chapter, did anyone come to mind that you need to forgive, or perhaps whose forgiveness you need to seek? If so, what's your next step?

_____
_____
_____
_____
_____
_____
_____

> *Repay no one evil for evil, but give thought to do what is honorable in the sight of all. If possible, so far as it depends on you, live peaceably with all. Beloved, never avenge yourselves, but leave it to the wrath of God, for it is written, "Vengeance is mine, I will repay, says the Lord." To the contrary, "if your enemy is hungry, feed him; if he is thirsty, give him something to drink; for by so doing you will heap burning coals on his head."*
>
> —Romans 12:17-20

Consider the scripture above and answer the following questions:

What do these verses reveal about forgiveness?

_____

_____

_____

_____

_____

Examine the relationship between our ability to forgive and our experience of God's forgiveness. How does the forgiveness we've received from God empower us to forgive others? Share insights from the text that highlight forgiveness as an integral part of our new nature.

_____

_____

_____

_____

_____

Reflect on the dangers of harboring bitterness and unforgiveness. How does bitterness affect the body, hormonal and immune systems, and contribute to various illnesses? Discuss the analogy of bitterness as a poisonous substance and its impact on one's well-being.

_____
_____
_____
_____
_____
_____
_____
_____
_____
_____

Explore the process of forgiveness and its connection to healing. Why is forgiveness a process, and how does it contribute to the healing of our hearts? Discuss the layers of forgiveness and the importance of being patient and tenacious in the journey of forgiveness.

_____
_____
_____
_____
_____
_____
_____
_____
_____
_____

Discuss the distinction between forgiveness and reconciliation. How is forgiveness a unilateral act, and why does reconciliation require both parties to move toward each other? Share examples from the text or personal experiences that illustrate the complexities of forgiveness and reconciliation.

_____
_____
_____
_____
_____
_____
_____
_____
_____
_____
_____

CHAPTER 23

HEALED FROM "NEXT."

Experience freedom from bondage to "next."

READING TIME

As you read Chapter 23: "Healed from "Next."" in *Enough.*, review, reflect on, and respond to the text by answering the following questions.

REVIEW, REFLECT, AND RESPOND:

Discuss the metaphor of the soul as a garden that needs tending. How does neglecting the garden of the soul lead to the growth of weeds like doubt and fear? How can a patient and attentive approach to spiritual well-being help prevent drought and maintain a healthy soul?

_____
_____
_____
_____
_____
_____
_____
_____

How would you define "destination addiction"?

_____
_____
_____
_____
_____
_____
_____
_____

What are some symptoms of destination addiction? What are the justifications we use in order to continue believing it's true?

___

What's the promise of "hurry sickness"? Why is it a sickness and not a virtue?

___

Examine the biblical truths presented regarding one's value, belonging, freedom from guilt and shame, security, and significance in Christ. How can these truths counteract the societal obsession with always looking to the future for validation and fulfillment? Share personal reflections on how these truths have influenced your perspective.

_____
_____
_____
_____
_____
_____
_____
_____
_____
_____

What would the pace of grace look like for you? For your family?

_____
_____
_____
_____
_____
_____
_____
_____
_____
_____
_____
_____

Consider the choice presented when the Spirit reveals areas where God's best may have been missed. How can individuals respond positively to the Spirit's guidance without succumbing to self-condemnation or defensiveness? Discuss the role of God's grace in empowering transformative choices and aligning with His agenda.

_____
_____
_____
_____
_____
_____
_____
_____
_____

As you read this book, what insights and revelations has God given you? How are you responding to them? What difference will they make over time?

_____
_____
_____
_____
_____
_____
_____
_____
_____

www.ingramcontent.com/pod-product-compliance
Lightning Source LLC
Chambersburg PA
CBHW062112080426
42734CB00012B/2839